The Wheels on the Bus

The Child's World®

Published in the United States of America by The Child's World®
1980 Lookout Drive • Mankato, MN 56003-1705
800-599-READ • www.childsworld.com

Acknowledgments
The Child's World®: Mary Berendes, Publishing Director
Editorial Directions: E. Russell Primm, Editor; Lucia Raatma, Proofreader
The Design Lab: Kathleen Petelinsek, Art Direction and Design;
  Anna Petelinsek and Victoria Stanley, Page Production

Library of Congress Cataloging-in-Publication Data
The wheels on the bus / illustrated by Ronnie Rooney.
      p. cm. — (Children's favorite activity songs)
Summary: Presents an illustrated version of the traditional song and a list of
matching movements.
   ISBN 978-1-60253-191-8 (library bound : alk. paper)
   1. Children's songs—Texts. [1. Folk songs. 2. Songs. 3. Buses—Songs and
music. 4. Finger play.] I. Rooney, Ronnie, ill. II. Title.
   PZ8.3.W575 2009
   782.42—dc22   2009001573
   [E]

ILLUSTRATED BY RONNIE ROONEY

The wheels on the bus
go round and round.
Round and round.
Round and round.

4

The wheels on the bus go round and round, all around the town!

The wipers on the bus
go *swish, swish, swish*!
Swish, swish, swish!
Swish, swish, swish!
The wipers on the bus
go *swish, swish, swish*,
all around the town!

6

The baby on the bus goes,
"*Wah, wah, wah.*"
"*Wah, wah, wah.*"
"*Wah, wah, wah.*"

The baby on the bus goes,
"*Wah*, *wah*, *wah*,"
all around the town.

The people on the bus
go up and down.
Up and down.
Up and down.

The people on the bus
go up and down,
all around the town.

The horn on the bus
goes *beep*, *beep*, *beep*!
Beep, *beep*, *beep*!
Beep, *beep*, *beep*!
The horn on the bus goes
beep, *beep*, *beep*, all around the town.

The money on the bus
goes *clink, clink, clink*!
Clink, clink, clink!
Clink, clink, clink!
The money on the bus goes *clink,*
clink, clink, all around the town.

SONG ACTIVITY

Move hands in a circular motion to these verses:
The wheels on the bus go round and round.
Round and round.
Round and round.
The wheels on the bus go round and round,

Extend arms up and out at the end of each stanza:
all around the town!

ADDITIONAL ACTIONS

Sway hands back and forth: *Swish, swish, swish!*

Rub eyes: *"Wah, wah, wah."*

Stand up and sit down: Up and down.

Pretend to beep a horn: *Beep, beep, beep!*

Pretend to drop coins in to pay: *Clink, clink, clink!*

BENEFITS OF NURSERY RHYMES AND ACTIVITY SONGS

Activity songs and nursery rhymes are more than just a fun way to pass the time. They are a rich source of intellectual, emotional, and physical development for a young child. Here are some of their benefits:

* Learning the words and activities builds the child's self-confidence—"I can do it all by myself!"

* The repetitious movements build coordination and motor skills.

* The close physical interaction between adult and child reinforces both physical and emotional bonding.

* In a context of "fun," the child learns the art of listening in order to learn.

* Learning the words expands the child's vocabulary. He or she learns the names of objects and actions that are both familiar and new.

* Repeating the words helps develop the child's memory.

* Learning the words is an important step toward learning to read.

* Reciting the words gives the child a grasp of English grammar and how it works. This enhances the development of language skills.

* The rhythms and rhyming patterns sharpen listening skills and teach the child how poetry works. Eventually the child learns to put together his or her own simple rhyming words— "I made a poem!"

ABOUT THE ILLUSTRATOR

Ronnie Rooney was born and raised in Massachusetts. She attended the University of Massachusetts at Amherst for her undergraduate study and Savannah College of Art and Design for her MFA in illustration. In the last three years, she moved to Georgia, got married, got a dog, and had a baby girl—in that order!

Ronnie has illustrated numerous books for children. She enjoys painting and drawing so much, she would paint and draw all day even if she didn't get paid for it. She hopes to pass this love of art on to her little girl.